ND AR QUIZ

ANTHONY SCHOOL
LIBRARY

Walt Disney

When Dreams Come True

by JoAnn DiFranco

DILLON PRESS, INC.   MINNEAPOLIS, MINNESOTA   55415

The author gratefully acknowledges the assistance of the archivist at Walt Disney Productions in reviewing the biography for accuracy.

Library of Congress Cataloging in Publication Data

DiFranco, JoAnn.
Walt Disney : when dreams come true.

(Taking part books)
SUMMARY: A biography of Walter Elias Disney, whose enormous successes as a creator of animated films, of nature films, and of theme amusement parks have brought people's dreams and fantasies to life.

1. Disney, Walt, 1901-1966—Juvenile literature. 2. Animators—United States—Biography—Juvenile literature. [1. Disney, Walt, 1901-1966. 2. Motion pictures—Biography] I. Title II. Series: Taking part.

NC1766.U52D5326 1985 791.43'092'4 [B] [92] 84-12173
ISBN 0-87518-281-X (lib. bdg.)

Dillon Press, Inc., 242 Portland Avenue South
Minneapolis, Minnesota 55415

Printed in the United States of America

1   2   3   4   5   6   7   8   9   10   91   90   89   88   87   86   85

Contents

 Walt Disney

When Walt Disney, celebrated filmmaker and entertainer, died in 1966, he left behind a lifetime of dreams to share with the world—dreams that began when he was a young Missouri farm boy. Born into a poor family where hard work left little time for play, Walt's first dream was to study art. His first artwork appeared at age seven when he took a bucket of tar and a brush and drew pictures of animals on the outside walls of the family farmhouse. The result of his efforts was a strapping from his father, but encouraged by an understanding aunt and a neighborly doctor, he continued his drawing.

A second dream for Walt began when, at fourteen, he began attending art classes. He wanted to be a cartoonist. In Kansas City he realized this dream when he was hired as a full-time cartoonist. Out of this cartooning experience came a third dream, that of filmmaker.

From cartoonist to filmmaker took Disney from Kansas City to California and Hollywood, the movie capital of the world. Disney's first major film success came in 1928 with the creation of Mickey Mouse in "Steamboat Willie."

Nine years later he completed the world's first full-length cartoon, *Snow White and the Seven Dwarfs*.

Following several other successful full-length cartoons, Disney had a new dream. Now he wanted to make other types of films. The 1940s and 1950s saw the arrival of Disney nature and live-action films. His greatest movie success was *Mary Poppins* (1964), which combined both live action and animation.

The success of these films pleased Walt, but, as always, he had a new dream. Next, he wanted to build an amusement park where families could do things together. In 1955, this dream came true with the opening of Disneyland in Anaheim, California.

Walt Disney never stopped dreaming. At the time of his death, he was already planning a second park, and this final dream, Walt Disney World, came true nearly five years after his death.

From a boy who loved to ride trains in the Midwest to a Hollywood filmmaker who had his own railroad in his yard, Walt Disney's life is one of dreams come true.

1/A Boy Dreams

Back home the first snowfall of winter has covered the ground, but in Florida at Walt Disney World, the season is always summer. Here horse-drawn trolleys roll down Main Street, past an old-fashioned ice cream parlor, a candy store, and a silent-movie theater. Nearby, a railroad train takes guests on a tour of the Magic Kingdom. Meanwhile, children and adults pass by Cinderella Castle, a graceful building with cone-shaped towers reaching toward the sky. The castle, right out of the world of make-believe, sets the mood for this special place.

Walt Disney World is a center of fun and magic for people of all ages. Children shriek happily as they cruise down alligator-filled rivers or spin around in giant Mad Hatter teacups. Adults stare in disbelief at lifelike, moving figures of United States presidents. Those who dare, line up for Space Mountain, a wild roller coaster ride. Others board a

monorail for a ride to EPCOT Center, where they will experience a few hours in the world of the future.

Amid the bustle of activity, life-size cartoon characters, Mickey Mouse, Donald Duck, and Goofy, walk about greeting visitors. Spending time in this magic place with its cartoon characters, rides, and adventures, is surely a dream come true. But this wonderland of fun is all the result of another dream, a life-long dream of a man named Walt Disney.

Walter Elias Disney was born in Chicago on December 5, 1901. His father, Elias, was the owner of a small construction company. His mother, Flora, helped with the business and often drew up the plans for the houses Elias built. Most of her time, however, was spent caring for her children. There were five Disney children in all, three brothers older than Walt and a younger sister.

The older Disney children helped to take care of the younger ones. Roy, who was eight years older than Walt, often pushed his brother's baby carriage. Through the years, Roy watched out for Walt and was always kind and generous to him. A special closeness grew between these two brothers, which lasted throughout their lives.

The Disney family was poor. Elias was a hard worker

who had tried many jobs, each time hoping to do well. But his dreams never worked out as he had planned. Before Walt was born, Elias had tried and given up several jobs. When the Chicago construction company began to fail, he moved his family once more. Elias thought country living would be a good change for them.

In 1906 the Disneys settled on a forty-five-acre farm in Marceline, Missouri. The two oldest sons did not like farm work and returned to Chicago the following year. Walt and his brother Roy were then left to help their parents with the farm chores. At the age of six, Walt was already beginning a life of hard work.

For the Disneys, life in the country was difficult. Running the farm was hard work, and Elias needed his family to help him. There was little time for playing. Most of the day the children were busy with farm chores. Elias gave them neither toys nor spending money. Gifts at Christmas were useful articles like socks and underwear. When the children displeased him, Elias punished them by hitting them with a strap.

Elias also worried about weather, crops, and earning enough money to care for his family. Once when the market

was poor, Elias, Flora, and Roy went door-to-door trying to sell baskets of apples. Sometimes the butter and eggs that should have been on the Disney table were sold to pay the bills.

In spite of the work and the demands of his strict father, Walt enjoyed the years on the farm. For fun he rode the backs of hogs, often ending the ride in a muddy puddle. When his chores were done, he found time to care for his pet piglet, Skinny, or to take a walk through the countryside. On hot days, he and Roy would walk miles to a creek for a cool dip.

Roy tried to make things more pleasant for his younger brother and sister. He was old enough to get extra jobs off the farm. With his own money, Roy sometimes treated the younger children to a present or with a visit to a carnival. Walt especially liked the carnival—a love that would stay with him throughout his life.

During the farm years, Walt became interested in drawing. One of his first works of art, unfortunately, got him into a real scrape. One day seven-year-old Walt dipped a brush into his father's tar barrel and drew large animals on the outside walls of the white farmhouse. When his father dis-

covered the pictures, he was angry and used the strap on him.

Although the Disney family was too busy with farm problems to pay attention to Walt's interest in art, his Aunt Margaret was more understanding. Shortly after the tar incident she came for a visit. As usual, she brought gifts with her, but this time she had something special for Walt. She gave him drawing paper and a box of crayons. During her stay, his aunt asked Walt to draw some pictures for her. She was pleased with his drawings, and her encouragement had a lasting effect on the young artist.

Fun-loving, old Doc Sherwood also encouraged Walt's artwork. He was Walt's "buddy," and together they enjoyed wild, fast rides in Doc's horse-drawn carriage. One day Doc asked Walt to sketch his favorite stallion, Rupert. Although the horse would not stay still, somehow Walt was able to finish the picture. Doc liked the drawing so much that he paid Walt a shiny new quarter for it. This encouragement first started Walt dreaming about studying art.

Walt's dream, however, would have to wait. The farm was in trouble. First the well went dry, and Elias had to dig another. Then the apple harvest was poor. Bad times

continued, and in 1909 Elias came down with pneumonia. Roy and young Walt could not run the farm alone. Along with these problems, Flora felt the farm would never be successful. Finally, she convinced Elias to give up the farm, and in 1910 it was sold. With the money he received from the sale, Elias bought a 700-customer newspaper route in Kansas City, Missouri.

Although Walt was only nine, he had to help his father and Roy deliver both the morning and the evening papers. For the next six years, his day began at three-thirty each morning. Many times he trudged through snow that was many feet deep. His father never allowed a paper to be thrown, and even in bad weather Walt had to walk up to the front door of every house.

Each morning Walt looked forward to his stops at apartment houses. Once inside he would run quickly from floor to floor, making his deliveries. Afterward, he would lie down in a warm hallway and rest for a few minutes. Walt also liked old houses with big porches where sometimes a toy was left out. Walt enjoyed sitting on the porch and pretending the toy was his for just a little while.

Roy and Walt were not paid for their work. Both boys

thought this was unfair, but Elias did not believe a father should pay his own sons for helping him. Even after Roy graduated from high school, Elias expected things to remain the same. At last Roy decided to leave home and work for himself. Once Roy left home, life was harder for Walt. He had to deliver more papers as well as do all the chores at home.

When Walt was able to get away from work, he would read stories or draw pictures. Once when his younger sister, Ruth, was sick, he amused her by drawing figures on pieces of paper. When he flipped the papers, the figures seemed to move. This was his very first attempt at animation, a way of making drawings come to life. Later in his life, this type of artwork would bring Walt great success.

Walt's schoolwork at the Benton Grammar School, however, was not very successful. The early morning paper route left him too tired to try hard in school. His teachers complained that he did not pay attention. But Walt did like the time set aside for drawing. In the fourth grade, he sketched flowers with human faces and hands. His teacher did not approve of his artwork, saying that Walt did not draw what he saw. Walt, however, liked the picture and

continued to do other drawings the same way.

At school, Walt's best friend was Walter Pfeiffer. The Pfeiffer home was always filled with activity, and Walt spent many happy hours there. Mr. Pfeiffer was a jolly man who told jokes and liked to gather his family and friends around the piano for an evening of singing.

The Pfeiffers took Walt and Walter to their first vaudeville show—a show filled with live singing, dancing, and comedy acts. Since Elias Disney would not have approved of his son watching vaudeville, Walt kept this outing a secret. Both Walt and his best friend loved the theater and the acts they saw there. The two thirteen year olds decided to put together an act of their own. They called themselves "The Two Walts." When the boys were given a chance to perform their act in a show, Walt had to sneak out his bedroom window.

Elias and Flora rarely went out in the evening. But one night they treated their daughter, Ruth, to a show at a neighborhood theater. They watched a performer stack three chairs and hold them high over his head. Imagine their surprise when they saw Walt sitting on the very top chair!

Walt liked show business, but his main interest was still

drawing. When he was fourteen, he asked his father for permission to attend Saturday classes at the Kansas City Art Institute. Elias agreed because he believed in anything that was educational. At the institute, Walt was finally able to study the subjects he liked. The classes he took included painting, drawing, and children's art. Now Walt not only wanted to study art, he began to consider art as a career. Walt was already thinking about becoming a cartoonist.

2/On His Own

In 1917 Elias Disney decided to move again. After selling the newspaper route, he returned to Chicago to become a part owner of a jelly factory. Walt did not go with the family right away. Instead, he stayed in Kansas City to finish the school term and to help the new owners of the paper route.

Walt's first taste of freedom came that June when he got a summer job as a candy butcher on the Missouri Pacific Railroad. As the train traveled between Missouri and Colorado, Walt walked among the passengers, selling newspapers, fruit, candy, and soda pop. Sometimes the engineer would let him climb into the coal car and ride along right behind the locomotive. How exciting it was for Walt to see the countryside go flying by! This love for trains stayed with him. Years later Walt included steam locomotives and passenger cars in his plans for Disneyland. As a grown man, he even had a miniature railroad built around his house.

At the end of the summer, Walt joined his family in Chicago. He attended McKinley High School where he did drawings for the school paper. After school, as he had always done as a youngster, he helped his father with the business. Now he worked in the jelly factory. But school and work did not stop him from finding time to study drawing. Three nights a week he went to classes at the Chicago Institute of Arts.

Art, however, was not the only thing on Walt's mind during that time. All over Chicago he saw men in military uniforms, who would soon be going overseas to fight in World War I. Everywhere there were bands playing, flags flying, and pretty girls calling to young men to "join up." Roy had joined the Navy, and Walt longed to do the same thing. But Walt was only sixteen, too young to enlist.

One day a friend told Walt that seventeen year olds were being accepted as Red Cross ambulance drivers. Here, Walt thought, was his chance. Elias did not like the idea and refused to help him. His mother, however, realized how badly Walt wanted to go. She said she would feel better knowing where he was rather than have him run away from home. His mother signed the papers and didn't say anything

when Walt wrote in his age as seventeen.

Walt was sent to Sound Beach, Connecticut, for training. When the war ended a few months after he enlisted, he was still at Sound Beach. Although he was glad for peace,

Walt felt sad at having missed his chance to see the world. There were, however, still wounded American soldiers in Europe, and ambulance drivers were needed there. To his surprise and delight, Walt was the last of fifty drivers chosen to go to France.

When Walt was not busy driving ambulances, he spent his free time drawing. Soldiers often asked for cartoons of themselves to send home. Walt sent some of his cartoons to magazines back home, but sadly, none were bought. Walt's pals, who often gave him ideas for the drawings, shared in his disappointment.

During his stay in France, Walt first earned money as an artist. Using oil paints, he decorated his jacket with a copy of a French medal. The men in the barracks wanted the design on their jackets, too. "Hey Diz, paint one for me," they called. He was paid ten francs, almost three dollars, for each one. This extra money, along with some of his regular pay, was sent home to his mother for safekeeping.

After eleven months in France, Walt returned home. A job was waiting for him at the jelly factory, but he had other plans. "I want to be an artist," he told his father. Elias saw no future in such a career, but Walt insisted on trying. He left his family and returned to his old hometown of Kansas City, where he hoped to be hired by one of America's greatest newspapers, *The Kansas City Star*.

Walt did not get a job on the *Star*, not even as an office boy. One of Roy's friends, however, got Walt an interview with the Pesmen-Rubin Commercial Art Studio. After working a week without pay, Walt was hired as an artist for fifty dollars a month. He would have earned twice that working at his father's jelly factory, but that didn't matter to Walt. He was happy that he had a job doing what he always wanted to do.

Aunt Margaret was the first person he told about his job. Walt never forgot that she was the one who had given him his first drawing materials years before. The little boy who had drawn tar pictures on a Missouri farmhouse had become an artist.

3/Success and Failure

Walt's first job as an artist lasted only six weeks. He worked during the busy Christmas season, but when business dropped off he lost his job. The experience was a good one, however, for he learned the tricks and shortcuts of the commercial artist. This type of artist does special drawings for customers who want to call attention to their products.

Another young man, Ub Iwerks, also worked for Pesmen-Rubin, and, like Walt, he also lost his job. The two of them decided to start a business of their own. Ub was a very talented artist who worked with Walt almost all of his life and shared in much of Disney's later success.

The two young men began their partnership by offering to do free artwork for a paper called the *Restaurant News* in return for a place to work. Walt asked his mother for the money he had sent home while he was in France. With the money she sent, Walt bought drawing boards and some art

supplies. Now he was ready for customers. In their first month, Walt and Ub earned more money than they would have at the jobs they had lost. The new company was a success.

Soon another opportunity called to Walt. The Kansas City Film Ad Company was looking for a full-time cartoonist. Walt went to the company's office with some of his cartoons, was offered the job, but really did not want to give up his own business. Ub, however, insisted that Walt take the job. Two months later, Ub was hired by the same company.

At their new job Walt and Ub received training in animation, which needs the skill of both an artist and photographer. The artist draws many pictures that are almost the same. In each picture there is a very slight change in the part of the picture where the artist wants movement. One by one the drawings are photographed. When all the still photos are flashed quickly on a movie screen, the sketched characters appear to move. Over fourteen hundred drawings are needed for a one-minute cartoon. A full-length movie cartoon makes use of over one million drawings and takes years to complete.

When Walt and Ub started at the Film Ad Company, full-length cartoons had not yet been made. Instead, they worked on one-minute cartoons. Walt, however, was not satisfied. He wanted to experiment and try new things. Talking his boss into lending him a camera, he started, on his own, to make short, special order, animated films. These he sold to movie theaters as fillers. Walt called them Laugh-o-Grams. Soon he was doing well enough to quit his job, buy his own camera, and again set up his own company.

The new project was off to a good start. In addition to the fillers, Walt sold six animated fairy tales, each seven minutes long. Ub Iwerks and the other assistants thought they had a bright future.

Unfortunately, their success did not last. Laugh-o-Grams was unable to collect for its films, and Disney had to let his staff go. Without money to pay his rent, he was forced to stay at his office. Sometimes the only meal he could afford was dry bread and beans. Even when Roy tried to help out by sending money, Walt was unable to get the business going again.

Although Walt's company failed, he was not discouraged. At the age of twenty-one, he had already known both

success and failure. Walt was ready to try again. A fresh start in a new place was all he needed, and he knew just the place. Selling his last possession, his camera, and tucking forty dollars into his pocket, he headed for Hollywood, the movie capital of the world.

In 1923, the year Walt arrived, there were several major movie studios in Hollywood. Putting aside his love for cartoons, Walt decided he would somehow get into the movie business. Any job, even sweeping floors, would have been fine. But no one hired him.

Finally, he decided that it was time to go back to what he knew best   cartooning. Convincing Roy to start a business with him, the brothers bought a camera and went to work. Animated cartoons were not new, but few were being made. The cartoons that had been made were short and poorly drawn. The studios did not see much future in animation. Walt knew that he would need an unusual idea and some good drawings if his work was to be noticed.

Walt decided to do his cartooning around a real girl. The result was a series of cartoons called Alice Comedies, which sold—but not very well. During this period, both brothers were eating a lot of beans. Finally, Ub Iwerks was sent for,

and with his help the "Alice" series started to do better.

As business picked up, other people were added to the staff. One was a young woman named Lillian Bounds. After work, Walt would sometimes drive Lillian home, where they would sit outside her house in his old car. Walt would never go in because he was ashamed of his shabby sweater and worn trousers. When the two decided to marry, Walt bought a new suit. He was so excited about his new clothes that when he was finally introduced to Lillian's family he blurted out, "How do you like my new suit?" The family approved of the suit and Walt, and the young couple was married in July, 1925.

In early 1926 the Disney brothers moved their work into a small studio on Hyperion Avenue, a few miles from downtown Los Angeles. By this time the company was known as the Walt Disney Studio. Before the year was out, the "Alice" series began to lose popularity. The time had come for something new. In 1927 the Disneys worked on a new series called Oswald the Lucky Rabbit. Everything went well, and the audiences liked Oswald. Pleased with his success, Walt and Lillian went to New York to renew the Oswald contract with the distributor, the person who bought the cartoons

and sent them to theaters around the country. The happy couple soon faced some unpleasant news.

In New York, Walt was offered less money for each cartoon. He refused to accept the amount, only to discover that the distributor owned the rights to the Oswald character. Since several Disney artists had already agreed to work for the distributor, the series could continue to be made— without Disney.

The experience was a painful one for Walt. He was upset that some of his artists would agree to work without him. He was also angry that a clever businessman could steal his work. But Walt learned a valuable lesson from this experience. In the future he would control all rights to his work.

The train ride back to Los Angeles was a long one for the Disneys. The steady sounds of the moving train relaxed Walt and helped him think. The chugging wheels, he said, seemed to talk to him. The word he heard was "mouse." In his mind he soon had an imaginary mouse dressed in red velvet pants with two huge white buttons. He named him Mortimer. The name sounded too formal to Lillian. She suggested "Mickey."

4/A Famous Mouse

Back in Hollywood, Iwerks and Disney brought Mickey to life. Iwerks drew the mouse—a round head, black button eyes, big ears, long skinny arms and legs, huge, white-gloved hands, and large feet. Disney gave him his cartoon role—a fun-loving character, who was always in trouble. Before the Disney studio began work on the first Mickey cartoon, Hollywood surprised the world. *The Jazz Singer*, the first motion picture with sound, was shown on October 6, 1927. No longer would moviegoers be content with silent movies.

Mickey Mouse had to greet the world with sound. Taking his work to New York, Walt talked to sound experts. Disney would provide the squeaky, high-pitched voice for Mickey—something he would continue to do for the next twenty years. An orchestra was hired to record the background music for the cartoons. When the soundtrack was added, Mickey Mouse was ready to meet the public.

On November 18, 1928, "Steamboat Willie," Mickey's first cartoon, was shown at the Colony Theater in New York. Of course, Walt was there waiting to see how the audience would respond. What he heard was happy laughter. Both Mickey and the sound cartoon were a tremendous success. More "Mouse" cartoons were soon demanded.

"Gallopin Gaucho," "Plane Crazy," and "The Barn Dance" followed quickly. Each cartoon was a hit, and Mickey Mouse was a star! Like live Hollywood actors, Mickey's name went up in lights above the theaters that showed his movies. Later, other characters, including Pluto and Goofy, were added to the mouse cartoons, and they, too, became stars in films of their own. One day, while Walt was listening to the radio, he heard Clarence Nash reciting, "Mary Had a Little Lamb" in a squawky voice. Walt hired Nash and created the hot-tempered Donald Duck to match the voice. Years later, Nash was a special guest at Donald's 50th birthday party. Like the other Disney characters, Donald had parts in Mickey's early films and later starred in films of his own.

Mickey soon became an American symbol. Many companies paid Walt to use Mickey's picture on their products.

A watch company with serious money problems put out Mickey Mouse watches, and their business was saved. Today the original Mickey Mouse watches are collectors' items. Mickey and his pals also appeared on everything imaginable, including children's notebooks, silverware, and cereal bowls. A cartoon strip for the newspapers was started in 1930. Even the queen of England chose Mickey Mouse china as gifts for hundreds of children.

The products and the Mickey Mouse films made their way all over the world. In every country where the films were shown, Mickey and his friends thrilled theater audiences. At home, Americans tried to pronounce his name as he was called in other countries. In Italy, Mickey was Topolino; in Japan, Mikki Kuchi; in Sweden, Musse Pigg; and in Argentina, El Ratón Mickey. In 1935 Roy and Walt traveled to Paris where Mickey was honored by the League of Nations, as an "international symbol of goodwill."

Throughout the years, Mickey's cartoons became better and better, but one thing always remained the same—Mickey himself. Walt watched over him and never allowed his artists or writers to change Mickey's personality. He told them, "Mickey's a nice fellow who never does anybody any

harm, who gets into scrapes through no fault of his own but always manages to come up grinning." In many ways Walt and Mickey were alike. Both liked adventure, and neither gave up when the going got rough. They both always tried to do their best.

While Mickey Mouse's popularity was soaring, Walt faced a new challenge—color. Up to this time a two-color process had been used to make some poor quality color films. In 1932 a new, and much better, three-color process called Technicolor was available. Walt wanted to be the first to try it. Roy thought it was too expensive and unnecessary and asked friends to try to talk Walt out of it. Instead, Walt talked Roy into going along with him!

"Flowers and Trees" caused a lot of excitement in the movie business. Walt Disney had put out a full-color cartoon! In addition, he had made a great business deal. Only the Disney studio could use the new Technicolor process in cartoons for the next two years. This move put Disney ahead of other cartoonmakers. Added to this success, in 1932 "Flowers and Trees" became the first Disney work and the first cartoon to win an Academy Award.

In 1933, "Three Little Pigs" opened at Radio City Music

Hall in New York. There, and later in theaters across America, the cartoon was called Disney's finest work so far. Audiences loved the pigs and hated the big bad wolf. The movie's theme song, "Who's Afraid of the Big Bad Wolf" was soon heard all over the country. Disney not only had a successful movie but also a song hit!

Soon after the success of "Three Little Pigs," Walt was honored by a group from *Parents' Magazine*. The people were about to present him with a special award when they realized he had left the room. The surprised group was told that Mr. Disney had to leave quickly for the hospital. There, Lillian Disney was about to present him with a different kind of award. Diane Disney, their first child, was born that day. Three years later another daughter, Sharon, completed the Disney family.

5/Disney's Folly

By experimenting with the Mickey Mouse cartoons, Walt had learned a lot about animation, color, sound, and photography. Now he felt ready to make a full-length cartoon movie. Walt even knew what story he wanted to film.

One evening Disney stood in front of several of his artists and began to act out the story of *Snow White*. He played all the parts including a dainty Snow White, several of the jolly dwarfs, a mean queen, and a charming prince. His one-person show took two hours. When he was finished, he turned to his audience and said, "That's going to be our first feature."

People in Hollywood soon heard about Disney's plan. They knew the kinds of problems he would have and were sure that this time Disney would fail. His latest project became known as "Disney's Folly," but Walt did not mind. As he had done many times before, he went ahead with his plan.

Snow White took five years to make. Walt checked over every part of the project and demanded work as perfect as possible. Staff members knew what he wanted and tried very hard to please him. During the *Snow White* years, Disney's staff grew to nearly one thousand people.

Walt would not allow any problem to stop him from completing *Snow White*. When banks were afraid to lend him the huge amounts of money he needed, Walt showed bits and pieces of the unfinished film to one of the bankers. When the showing was over, the banker told Walt that his film was sure to make a lot of money. He then arranged for Walt to get the money he needed.

Costing more than a million dollars, the movie was finally completed. *Snow White and the Seven Dwarfs* had its first showing on December 21, 1937. The audience at the Carthay Circle Theater in Los Angeles was filled with Hollywood stars. For eighty-three minutes they laughed and cried at this fairy tale, which came alive on the screen. When the film ended, the audience stood up and cheered.

The world's first full-length cartoon was a super success! At New York's Radio City Music Hall, the film ran for weeks. The film's songs, "Heigh-Ho," "Whistle While You

Walt Disney World in Orlando, Florida, is a Disney dream come true.

(Above) *Mickey Mouse and his friends greet visitors to Walt Disney World.* (Right) *The cone-shaped towers of Cinderella Castle rise above the center of the Magic Kingdom.*

Donald Duck makes friends with a young visitor at the entrance to the Magic Kingdom (left). *In Adventureland* (above), *mechanical elephants spray water on each other. (Walt Disney World)*

Walt Disney created Mickey Mouse and introduced him to movie-goers in 1928. In the 1930s, Mickey appeared in print as well as on the screen and soon became an international symbol.

In 1949, Walt took his wife, Lillian, and daughters, Diane and Sharon, (above), *to England to watch the filming of his first live-action movie,* Treasure Island. *In Hollywood, Walt* (right) *proudly holds four Oscars that he was awarded in 1954.*

On July 17, 1955, Walt Disney (left) *sat in front of Sleeping Beauty Castle during a telecast of the official opening of Disneyland. A horseback rider himself, Walt Disney fondly pets the nose of a Disneyland horse* (above).

At Disneyland, the Mark Twain *riverboat* (left) *steams around the bend for a journey down the Rivers of America in Frontierland.* (Above) *The Disneyland speedy monorail takes visitors into worlds of fun and fantasy.*

45

At EPCOT Center, the colorful rainbow corridor is just one of the striking attractions in the Journey into Imagination pavilion.

At sunset, the view from the Japanese pavilion on the shore of the World Showcase Lagoon is breathtaking. (EPCOT Center)

The gleaming silver ball, Spaceship Earth, is a splendid sight, day and night, at EPCOT Center.

Work," and "Someday My Prince Will Come" were heard on radios across the country. People who had called the idea "Disney's Folly" were further surprised when *Snow White* won a special Academy Award that year.

The success of *Snow White* encouraged Walt. He wanted to do other feature films, but, first, he needed a new studio. The Hyperion Avenue studio was overcrowded.

Walt planned for the new studio in Burbank to be modern and attractive. Walt's idea was to give his staff everything they needed to do their best work and to make them comfortable and happy during working hours. Built like a tiny city, the studio had many buildings and wide lawns. There was a restaurant, a lounge, and a gym. Offices were large and well lighted and contained the best equipment. The studio had a theater, three stages, and a laboratory for experiments in new film methods. At the Burbank studio there was enough room to work on several projects at once.

In 1940, fifteen hundred people worked at the Burbank studio. Three projects kept everyone busy. The first, *Pinocchio,* was the story of a wooden puppet who came to life. This film introduced a popular Disney character, Jiminy

Cricket, Pinocchio's conscience. Two popular songs from the movie, "When You Wish Upon a Star" and "Give a Little Whistle," were added to the list of Disney music successes.

Fantasia, the second film, was made up of seven different animated parts. The background music for each part was a well-known piece of music written by a famous composer. The artists tried to capture the feel and mood of the music in their drawings. Nothing like *Fantasia* had ever been tried, but, unfortunately, the experiment was not successful. Special sound systems set up in the theaters for *Fantasia* were expensive, and many theaters could not show the film. Years later, the film was again shown in the theaters, which now had better sound systems. This time the film did well. Today experts agree that some of the finest animation ever done appears in *Fantasia*.

Walt's third project was *Bambi*, a film with beautiful nature scenes. Special art classes, with live deer as models, helped the artists do the drawings for this film.

The three new Disney films were enjoyed by the public, but none of them had the same success as *Snow White*. Next, Walt decided to make a shorter and less expensive film. His staff worked on *Dumbo*, the story of a large-eared

baby elephant who discovers he can fly. Audiences liked the film, and it brought some much needed money into the studio.

In May 1941, many of the workers at the Walt Disney Studio went on strike. The studio employed hundreds of workers, and they wanted a union to protect their jobs. For Walt to see his people carrying picket signs in front of the studio upset him. He needed to get away from the nightmare of the strike.

Walt got a chance to get away and still continue to work in the film business. The United States government asked him to go on a goodwill tour of South America. In Argentina, Brazil, and Chile, crowds followed him everywhere. The South American people had known and loved Mickey, Donald, and their friends for many years, and now they welcomed the man who had created them. As Walt traveled, he filmed many of the things he saw. When he returned home, he made an animated film called, *Saludos Amigos*, which was popular in both the United States and South America.

During the time Walt was in South America, the strike had been settled. Walt was not angry with his workers

because he felt they had done what they thought was right. All he wanted now was for everyone to work together in making more films.

World War II caused a new problem for the Disney studio. Immediately following the bombing of Pearl Harbor on December 7, 1941, the army took over the studio. The army had chosen the Disney studio because it could be closed up tight, with no light showing from the outside. That way the building could still be used, even during a blackout. Walt and his workers had to wear special badges to get in and out of the studio's gates while the sound stage was turned into a machine shop where army equipment was repaired. Walt said he didn't mind the disorder and found the army's presence kind of exciting. The army remained at the studio for seven months.

Once the army left, Walt started making films for the government. Some were training films for soldiers, but others were shown in local movie theaters. One called "The New Spirit" starred Donald Duck and explained to Americans that their tax money was important to winning the war.

In the years following the war, the Disney studio continued to put out short cartoons. Work was also started on

new full-length, animated films. Cartoons, however, were no longer enough for Walt. Now he wanted to get into other types of films. Photographers were sent to Alaska to film animal life, and the film they shot, *Seal Island,* was used to begin a new series called True-Life Adventures. A crew was also sent to England to film Disney's first live-action movie, *Treasure Island.* Walt and his family also traveled to England to watch the filming.

Walt's family was always an important part of his life. During the 1940s and 1950s Walt put in long, hard days at the studio and looked forward to quiet evenings at home with Lillian and his daughters. When he was a boy, Walt had little time to play. Now he liked to relax in his own home and watch his children playing with the special toys he gave them. He not only watched, but often he joined right in and played with them.

Despite Walt's busy schedule, he took an active role in raising his children. Walt drove his daughters to school, to birthday parties, and to dancing lessons. He taught them how to swim and to ride horseback. When they were older, Walt taught them to drive a car in the studio's parking lot. He also kept Diane and Sharon away from photographers

who often followed the children of famous parents. When the girls were young, they did not know their father was a well-known Hollywood figure. Later, Diane complained to her father, "You never told me you were Walt Disney!"

When the Disney family looked for land for a new house, Walt insisted on plenty of space. Lillian, knowing of his love for trains, guessed what he wanted to do. The Disney home was built on Carolwood Drive in Holmby Hills, and Walt's miniature train was built right on the property! The railroad was called the Carolwood-Pacific. Walt's favorite pastime was to put on his coveralls and engineer's cap and take his daughters and their friends for a ride.

The miniature railroad sparked another idea. Walt's children enjoyed the train rides, but other parents had few places to take their children for a day of fun. There were amusement parks, but most of them were poorly cared for and often dreary looking. Besides, there was little for adults and children to do together in these parks. Walt started dreaming about building his own amusement park.

6/When Dreams Come True

The 1950s and 1960s were very busy years for Walt Disney. His studio turned out several new full-length cartoons. *Cinderella, Alice in Wonderland, Peter Pan, Lady and the Tramp*, and *Sleeping Beauty* charmed audiences the same way *Snow White* had done years before. While some of the staff worked on cartoons, other people worked on live-action films. Besides *Treasure Island*, the Disney studio put out children's classics, *The Sword and the Rose* and *The Story of Robin Hood and His Merrie Men*. In 1954, *20,000 Leagues Under the Sea* was completed, which was Walt's first film starring major Hollywood stars. Other Disney films with other stars included *Swiss Family Robinson, The Shaggy Dog, The Absent-Minded Professor*, and *Pollyanna*. In 1964, *Mary Poppins* made film history and became Walt Disney's greatest movie success. The movie combined both live action and animation, and the songs as

well as the special effects delighted audiences and critics. The film was considered for thirteen Academy Awards, and Julie Andrews, who played Mary Poppins, was named the best actress of the year.

Longer nature films were also made. The most popular were *The Living Desert*, *The Vanishing Prairie*, and *The African Lion*. For these projects, Disney pushed his staff the same way he had on all the animation projects. He expected work that was perfect. Photographers were given the best equipment and plenty of time. Special camera lenses made it possible for them to film animals that were over a mile away while up close they could film the tiniest of insects.

The success of the nature films pleased Walt. There was, however, something about films, all types of films, that bothered him. Once a film was finished and shown in the theaters, nothing more could be done with it. Nothing could be changed or added. Walt now wanted to work with something live, something that would never be finished, and something that could become more and more beautiful. He wanted to build an amusement park. His dream park already had a name, Disneyland.

Walt was determined to build Disneyland. He had never

before been talked out of a project he really wanted to do. All his life he did things that others thought were impossible. First, Walt set up an organization called WED (the initials of his name) to start planning the park. Roy warned him that he would have trouble getting money to start construction. Walt did not agree. "Television," he told Roy was the answer to his money problem.

By the 1950s, television was an important part of American life. Walt was sure that the people who went to theaters to see Disney films would now watch his work on television. He made a deal with the American Broadcasting Company to do a television show for them if they would help with the money for his amusement park. In 1954 a contract was signed, and Walt's television career began.

Although Walt said he was scared to death, he bravely stood in front of the cameras and, week after week, introduced his television show, "Disneyland." The hit of the first season was a series entitled *Davy Crockett*, tales of a backwoods hero. A song written for the show, "The Ballad of Davy Crockett" was the number one song in the country for weeks. Children all over America began wearing coonskin caps and carrying toy Crockett rifles. The Crockett craze

swept the country just as the Mickey Mouse craze had in the 1930s.

Another popular Disney television show was "The Mickey Mouse Club." Every afternoon between five and six o'clock, most of the TV sets in America were tuned in to this show. The soon-to-become famous Mouseketeers, children wearing caps shaped like Mickey Mouse ears, sang and danced as part of the entertainment. Old Disney cartoons were shown as well as newsreels of children in foreign countries and stories from children's books, like *The Hardy Boys.*

Disney's movies of the '50s and '60s and his television shows proved that he was much more than a great cartoon-maker. He was also an entertainer. Any film made by Disney for the movies or for television promised fine family entertainment. Throughout the world he was honored as a master filmmaker. In his lifetime he received thirty-one Academy Awards. This award is one of the highest honors that filmmakers can give each other.

Once Walt Disney had achieved his goals as a movie-maker, all his energy was poured into plans for Disneyland. Walt did not care about costs. Everything had to be built just the way he had planned it in his mind. Every attraction, he said, must please the people. He knew the public expected the best from him, and that is what he planned to give them.

Disneyland, located in Anaheim, California, opened on July 17, 1955. Thirty thousand guests entered the park and walked down Main Street, USA, towards Sleeping Beauty Castle. From there they went on to the other four sections of the park. In Frontierland the *Mark Twain* riverboat stood ready to take visitors for a ride past Tom Sawyer Island. Tomorrowland offered a glimpse into the future and Adventureland, a look at the wonders of nature. In Fantasyland the guests escaped into the world of Disney cartoon characters.

For years Walt had waited for the day his dream park would be filled with people. With happy, laughing children and adults everywhere, Walt told a reporter, "Disneyland will never be completed as long as there is imagination left in the world."

During the next few years, Walt's imagination kept his park growing. Disneyland was a success beyond Walt's dreams and still he wanted improvements made. New attractions and rides were added. Attention was paid to tiny

details that would add pleasure to the visits made by millions of people. Everything was kept clean and attractive. During the evening hours, crews were busy repairing and painting. Walt insisted that nothing should ever look worn or old. He also insisted that all who worked in the park be polite and have a smile for everyone.

Although Disneyland was a dream come true for Walt, he never stopped dreaming. In 1958 he started planning another park, which, he insisted, would not be a copy of the first. This time he wanted to build a complete vacationland. Enough land was bought in Orlando, Florida, to build motels, hotels, and campgrounds. The new park would have many of the rides and attractions that were popular in Disneyland, as well as many others. Walt was especially excited about EPCOT, an experimental city of the future, which was going to be part of the Florida park.

Sadly, Walt Disney did not live to see his second theme park completed. Shortly after his sixty-fifth birthday, he went into the hospital, striken by cancer. Although he was very weak, he enjoyed visits with his wife and daughters and with his brother. The night before he died, Walt and Roy sat in the hospital room, talking about the new park and the

plans for EPCOT. Walt Disney died on December 15, 1966.

Following Walt's death, Roy Disney took over for his brother. Although he was seventy-three years old and wanted to retire, Roy said he wouldn't quit until he finished Walt's dream.

On October 31, 1971, Walt Disney World in Orlando, Florida, was opened to the public. The Disney family, including Lillian, Diane and Sharon and their families, and Roy and his family, attended the opening ceremonies. They all agreed that the park was everything that Walt had wanted it to be. Walt's final dream had come true.

Today, Walt Disney and his dreams live on. Millions of people every year visit Disneyland, Walt Disney World, and EPCOT Center. In Hollywood, Walt Disney Productions continue to make Disney films, which maintain Walt's high standards of excellence. Meanwhile, the magic of his early films keeps returning to movie theaters across the country. Here young audiences are as thrilled with the Disney cartoon characters as their parents and grandparents had been many years before when the name Walt Disney was new. The world shares, now and for years to come, Disney's dreams come true.

 *Glossary*

Academy Award—yearly awards given to people in the film industry for outstanding achievement

animation—a way of making motion-picture cartoons from a series of drawings

candy butcher—a person who sells food and reading materials on a train

cartoon—a drawing or a series of drawings that tells a story

cartoonist—a person who draws cartoons

comedy—a funny show with a happy ending; humorous entertainment

commercial artist—an artist who does special drawings for people who use them to call attention to their products

contract—a written understanding between two or more people to do or not do something; a written promise

distributor (movie)—a person who buys movies and sends them to theaters around the country

fillers—very short films sold to movie theaters to fill in spots before the feature show

live-action film—a film that uses real people or animals to act out a story

rights—something a person has a claim to

sound track—the area on a motion-picture film that carries the sound record

Technicolor—a process for making colored motion pictures

vaudeville—a show filled with live singing, dancing, and comedy acts

# Index

The Author

For author JoAnn DiFranco, writing about Walt Disney was an enjoyable experience, which recalled pleasant childhood memories. "As a child and honorary Mouseketeer with my own Mickey Mouse ears, I never dreamed I'd one day write about the man responsible for the many happy TV hours given to me and so many other children."

Ms. DiFranco is an English instructor at Holy Trinity Diocesan High School in Hicksville, New York. With her brother, Anthony, she is the co-author of *Mister Rogers: Good Neighbor to America's Children.* A mother of four sons, who enjoy many of the Disney cartoons and films that she herself treasured as a child, Ms. DiFranco makes her home in Oyster Bay, New York.